Wolf Hill

Remote Control

D1341192

Roderick Hunt

Illustrated by Alex Brychta

Oxford University Press

OXFORD

UNIVERSITY PRESS

Great Clarendon Street, Oxford OX2 6DP

Oxford New York
Athens Auckland Bangkok Bogotá Buenos Aires Cape Town
Chennai Dar es Salaam Delhi Florence Hong Kong Istanbul Karachi
Kolkata Kuala Lumpur Madrid Melbourne Mexico City Mumbai Nairobi
Paris São Paulo Shanghai Singapore Taipei Tokyo Toronto Warsaw

and associated companies in Berlin Ibadan

Oxford is a registered trade mark of Oxford University Press

© text Roderick Hunt 1999
© illustrations Alex Brychta
First Published 1999
Reprinted 2000, 2001
ISBN 0 19 918742 8

Printed in Hong Kong

Chapter 1

Every Sunday Gizmo's dad plays football. He plays for a team called Wolf Hill Wanderers.

Gizmo likes football, but he can't play very well. He has bad asthma. He always has his inhaler with him. If he runs a lot, he gets wheezy.

In any case, Gizmo is not much good at ball games. He can't kick a ball very hard. He can't catch. Throw a ball at Gizmo and he often drops it.

But Gizmo likes to watch his dad on Sundays.

'Wanderers are playing at home on Sunday,' Gizmo told Andy, Chris and Kat. 'Are you going to come and watch?'

'Okay,' said Kat.

'Me, too,' said Andy.

So on Sunday, Andy, Kat and Arjo went to watch Wanderers play. They were playing a team called A.B. Plastics.

Gizmo was excited. It was the quarter-final of the league.

There was trouble at the match. It ended with Mr Harding in hospital.

Chapter 2

The red socks caused the trouble.

Each week Mr Harding washes the team strip. The strip is a white top and white shorts. It has red socks. The top has a red flash. The shorts have a red stripe down the side.

That week, Mr Harding was busy. He couldn't wash the strip. Mrs Harding was away so she couldn't either.

Mr Harding spoke to Gizmo. 'Can you use the washing machine?'

'Of course I can,' said Gizmo.

'Right,' said Mr Harding. I want you to wash the team strip. The shirts are really muddy. You'd better use a hot wash.'

So Gizmo put the shirts and shorts in the washing machine. There was room for the red socks. He put them in too.

The red ran out of the socks. It turned everything pink.

'Oh no!' gasped Gizmo when he saw the pink shirts and shorts. He showed them to his dad. 'What have I done wrong?' he asked.

'It's my fault,' said Mr Harding. 'I should have told you not to put the socks in.'

'I feel terrible,' said Gizmo.

Chapter 3

Something else went wrong, too.

It was a cold day on Sunday. There had been a frost. Maybe the ground was too hard. Maybe the game should have been called off. But it wasn't.

A.B. Plastics came in a bus. They had about forty supporters.

The Wanderers were waiting. They were waiting for Mr Harding.

'Where's our strip?' someone shouted. 'We should have kicked off by now.'

A.B. Plastics started to sing. They sang, 'Why are we waiting? Oh, why are we waiting?' Their breath made clouds of steam in the cold air.

At last Mr Harding turned up. He handed out the pink shirts and shorts. 'Why are they pink?' shouted someone.

'I'm sorry,' said Mr Harding. 'The red socks got put in with the whites. It was an accident.'

There was nothing for it. The team had to play in a pink strip.

When A.B. Plastics saw them, they cheered. One of them called out, 'We like the new strip, lads!'

Gizmo was upset. He told Andy and Kat what had happened 'I washed the strip,' he said. 'How was I to know the red would run?'

Chapter 4

The game started. Wanderers won the toss. They kicked off. A cheer went up. Someone shouted, 'Change your lipstick. It doesn't match your pink kit.'

It was all too much for Wanderers.
The late start. The jokes about the
pink kit. They felt on edge. Some of
them were angry.

Gizmo sensed the mood. He
hopped from one foot to the other.

When Wanderers play, they always shout a lot. They shout to get the ball. 'Jason! Over here,' they shout, or, 'Steve! Steve! To me!'

In this game, they shouted more than ever. Why? It was because of the pink strip. It was because they were in a bad mood.

Wanderers played badly. They tackled too hard. They ran into players. They tripped them up and crashed into them. A.B. Plastics didn't like it. It was an ugly start to the game.

The referee stopped the match. 'Settle down, lads,' he said. 'Someone's going to get hurt.'

Ten minutes later, someone *did* get hurt - Gizmo's dad.

Chapter 5

Things didn't get better. First, A.B.
Plastics had the ball. Then, Wolf Hill
Wanderers had it.

Mr Harding plays on the wing. He's a big, heavy man. He doesn't run very fast. He's hard to tackle. Once he has the ball, he keeps it.

Mr Harding shouted. The ball flew towards him. He trapped the ball with his chest. It dropped to his feet. Then he began his slow, heavy run.

A.B. Plastics couldn't get the ball. Players charged Mr Harding. They bounced off him. He ran on. He ran towards the goal area.

'Shoot, Dad!' shouted Gizmo.

Two players thumped into Mr Harding. His legs went sideways. He crashed to the ground. There was a loud crack. Everyone gasped. The referee blew his whistle.

'Foul!' everyone shouted. 'It's a penalty.'

Mr Harding didn't get up. It looked as if he were in pain. His leg was twisted under him.

'Call an ambulance,' somebody shouted. 'I think he's broken his leg.'

That was when some of the players began to fight.

Chapter 6

Mr Harding lay on the pitch in agony. The referee stopped the game. 'This match is abandoned,' he said. 'I don't expect bad play like this.'

Gizmo ran on to the pitch. Mr Harding groaned. 'Oh Dad!' said Gizmo, 'Your leg looks bad.'

Gizmo was upset. His dad had broken his leg. He had to go to hospital. Gizmo went with him. Andy and Kat went home. 'Will you be all right, Gizmo?' said Kat before they went.

That evening Mr Harding was back home. His leg was in plaster. Luckily it wasn't a bad break. 'But I'll be off work for six weeks,' he said.

'Look what happens when I'm not there,' said Mrs Harding.

'I didn't mean to break my leg,' said Mr Harding.

'No, I mean these pink strips,' said Mrs Harding. She held up a pair of pink shorts. 'They're completely ruined.'

Mr Harding pulled a face. 'Don't mind about me,' he said. 'I suppose I don't matter.'

Mrs Harding gave him a hug. 'Well, you can do all your paper work,' she said.

'Thanks for nothing,' laughed Mr Harding.

Chapter 7

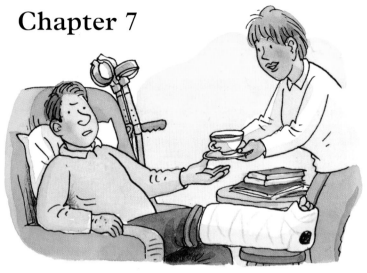

Gizmo's mum and dad have a shop. They sell electrical goods. Mrs Harding had to run the shop by herself.

Mr Harding didn't do his paper work. He didn't do anything. For a day or two, he was bad tempered. 'I'd rather be at work,' he moaned.

'I wish you'd stop moaning,' said Mrs Harding. 'I wish you'd find something to do.'

Mr Harding did. He made a model helicopter from a kit.

The helicopter was powered by an electric motor. It had a radio control.

Gizmo told everyone at school. 'My dad's making a model helicopter,' he said. 'I'm helping him.'

Chapter 8

It took Mr Harding a week to make the helicopter. Nobody saw much of Gizmo.

One day Andy, Kat and Chris went to play with Gizmo. They saw the helicopter. It was black with red markings. It looked really good.

'It's a Hyperfly,' said Gizmo. 'It has an AP29 electric motor.'

'It's brilliant,' said Andy. 'Why don't you start it up?'

Gizmo shook his head. 'No, too dangerous,' he said. He pointed to the rotor blades. 'Dad says they could take your head off.'

Then Gizmo showed them a black plastic box. It had an aerial and two little joysticks.

'This is the remote control,' said Gizmo. 'It's an Attack 2 radio.' He pushed a joystick with his thumb. The rotor blades on the helicopter tilted. The motor made a little buzzing noise.

Gizmo's dad was outside. He heard the noise and shouted, 'Don't touch that. I don't want you messing it up.'

But the next day Gizmo did touch it. He had to fly the helicopter by himself.

Chapter 9

'I want to see how the helicopter flies,' said Mr Harding. 'We'll go to Wolf Hill Park.'

Mrs Harding took him in the car. Gizmo, Andy and Kat went, too.

Mrs Harding drove up the hill. Then she stopped the car.

From the hill you could see Wolf Hill Wanderers' football club. You could look down on the clubhouse.

The clubhouse had changing rooms
and a bar. Mr Harding had helped
to build it. He had put in the wiring
and fixed up the lighting.

Mrs Harding had helped, too. She
had helped paint the clubhouse.

Mrs Harding began to walk down
the hill. She had the clubhouse keys.
'I'm going down to check the lights
are off,' she said. 'I won't be long.'

'Don't you want to watch the helicopter?' asked Gizmo.

'I'll watch it from the clubhouse,' said Mrs Harding. 'It will be safer down there.'

But she was wrong. It wasn't safe at all.

Chapter 10

'Now keep well back,' ordered Mr Harding.

He started the helicopter. The rotor blades turned faster and faster. The helicopter made a noise like an electric fan. Gizmo's face was red with excitement. His glasses slipped to the end of his nose.

The helicopter took off. It went up quite high. Then it circled round above the park. Mr Harding flew it over the football club.

Mrs Harding had reached the clubhouse. She looked up and waved. There was a motor-bike outside the club. She stopped to look at it. Then she went inside.

Mr Harding brought the helicopter back at full speed. Then he slowed it down. The helicopter came in low. Then it banked away again. Up, up it went - higher and higher.

Andy and Kat watched the helicopter.

Gizmo watched his dad. He kept watching the remote control. 'It looks easy to fly, Dad,' he said.

Then they heard the scream. It came from a long way off. It came from the clubhouse.

Gizmo's face went white.

The scream came from his mum.

Chapter 11

Two people ran out of the football club. One of them had a bag. They ran to the motor-bike and jumped on.

Mr Harding gasped. 'That was Ann who screamed!' he shouted. 'Quick!'

He dropped the remote control. Then he began to hobble down the hill on his crutches.

The helicopter hung in the air. Slowly it began to spin. It spun faster and faster. It was dropping out of the sky.

Gizmo picked up the remote control. 'Dad! Come back!' he shouted. Then he ran after his dad.

Down at the clubhouse the motor-bike wouldn't start. At last it roared into life. It sped across the football pitch.

The motor-bike was almost at the road. Then a police car turned in to Wanderers. The motor-bike skidded round. It roared back across the pitch. The police car chased it.

The bike slowed. It was making for the ditch. It went over like a scramble bike. The police car stopped. It couldn't jump the ditch. The bike roared across the park.

'They're getting away,' shouted Andy.

'Not if I can help it,' said Gizmo.

Chapter 12

Mr Harding lay on the ground. He had fallen over. His face was pale.

The helicopter was about to crash. 'Oh no!' groaned Mr Harding. Gizmo pointed the remote control. He moved the joysticks.

The helicopter rocked from side to side. It bucked and rolled. It looked as if it would crash. Then it flew straight.

Gizmo took the helicopter up. Then he brought it round. He flew it across the park. It went straight towards the motor-bike.

Suddenly the motor-bike rider saw
the helicopter. He braked hard. The
bike skidded. The back kicked
sideways. The riders fell off and slid
along the grass.

'Got them!' said Gizmo.

The police ran across to the bike. The riders got up, but they were too shaken to run. Andy and Kat cheered.

Mrs Harding came out of the clubhouse. She was waving at Mr Harding and shouting something.

Gizmo was trying to control the helicopter. Suddenly, it bucked and crashed into a tree.

Chapter 13

'Fancy running down hill with a broken leg!' said Mrs Harding.

Andy, Kat and Gizmo sat in the clubhouse. Mrs Harding had made everyone a cup of tea. Mr Harding still looked very pale.

'You screamed,' said Mr Harding.
'We thought you were in trouble.'

'I screamed to scare them,' said
Mrs Harding. 'They'd broken into
the fruit machines. They were putting
the money into a bag.'

She pointed to a broken window.
'That's how they got in,' she said. 'I
screamed at them and they ran away.'

'How about the police?' asked Kat.

'That was a bit of luck,' said Mrs
Harding. 'I phoned them up. There
was a patrol car in the area. It was
here in a few seconds.'

'It was lucky the bike wouldn't
start,' said Andy.

'Gizmo is the hero,' said Mr
Harding. 'The way he flew the
helicopter - straight at the
motor-bike.'

Gizmo grinned.

'By the way,' said his dad. 'What happened to the helicopter? I didn't see it land.'

Chapter 14

Gizmo looked upset. 'Sorry, Dad,' he said. 'I tried to land it but my hands were shaking. I couldn't control it.'

Mr Harding looked at Gizmo. 'It doesn't matter,' he said. 'I'm really proud of you. Maybe we'll build another one.'

'Can we make a radio control car instead?' asked Gizmo. 'Then all my friends can have a go.'

Mrs Harding smiled. 'His plaster comes off next week,' she said. 'Then he's back at work. You'll have to wait until he breaks his leg again.'

'I won't break it playing football,' said Mr Harding. 'I'm giving up.'

'That's your excuse,' laughed Mrs Harding. 'You just don't like wearing pink.'